The
Dream Catcher

Vol. 1

P.A.W.S.™

101 Steps

A Catalyst for Change

Faith McCune
&
June Davidson

DEDICATION

To all who have dreams unattained,
let no one keep them at bay.
As long as there is breath in you,
that dream is a heartbeat away.

To my husband, Bernard,
my greatest supporter and best friend,
and my dogs,
Prince, Pico, Blossom, John Boy, Duffy, Corrie,
and Danna, the best life coaches ever.

Faith McCune

FOREWORD

It is a real honor to write the foreword for this wonderful book, *The Dream Catcher, PAWS™ 101 Steps, A Catalyst for Change*, by Faith McCune and June Davidson.

This book is rich with ideas and concepts, some of which you can carry with you the rest of your life. Your heart will enlighten, smiles will form, but most importantly, your life will be enriched. Faith and June utilize a sense of playfulness to illustrate our limitless possibilities when we allow positive changes into our lives with the support of our furry friends.

Faith and June show you a way to live your life to its fullest. Their words share an inherent part of the quality of life and love. These qualities are transmitted through their words and experienced through our canine friends. Dogs allow us to dispel long-held misguided beliefs we hold as "total truths," when we receive the "pure innocence" of compassion, trust, and unconditional love from our canine friends.

Our pets bestow many precious gifts to help us heal ourselves by showering us with unconditional love. Faith and June remind us to treasure these precious gifts and to treasure our pets' lives for it is in those moments that we will be forever changed.

Faith and June are such extraordinarily gifted writers, speakers and healers. They help transform lives by revealing the true meaning and roles of our furry friends. They bring us back to the basic concept of learning unconditional love and compassion for ourselves and others. Their book brings us comfort and helps us realize what is truly important in life, and the simple act of reading *The Dreamcatcher, PAWS™ 101 Steps, A Catalyst for Change* will help you heal and grow.

Faith and June, thank you for this inspirational and life-altering book. It is a privilege to contribute my thoughts here.

With much respect and gratitude,
Dr. Christina Charbonneau
Award-winning doctor, certified coach, media personality, speaker and former medical school professor.

ACKNOWLEDGMENTS

June Davidson is an extraordinary person. Faith was very fortunate to meet her. Their first moments together were serendipitous. They were at a business conference. Faith arrived very early and saw June sitting in the lobby alone, enjoying the morning. Faith decided to introduce herself and, in that moment, her life changed. June awakened Faith to potential she never knew she had. But, it was the spirit of love and friendship that June conveyed that placed new purpose and courage in Faith to make the journey toward her dream. It is an honor to share June's talent and wisdom in this book.

CONTENTS

1 INTRODUCTION

In our early adult years, we make friends, marry, have children, buy a home or move to another state. These were exciting times, filled with wonder and adventure. We were nervous about the changes, but we didn't fear them. As we age, we become more vulnerable to unexpected or unpleasant changes. Friends move on or die, we divorce or lose a spouse or a job, children leave to start their own lives, technology passes us by, we suffer through a traumatic event, our health takes a downturn. Some of us don't marry and don't have children. Or, we lose a loving and faithful companion. When faced with these changes, one or many of these emotions come into play:

- Loneliness, abandonment
- Heartbreak, mistrust
- Unrelenting guilt
- Lack of support and understanding
- Isolation, exclusion
- Crippling memories that keep you from moving on

If you cannot reclaim your once-happy life on your own, it's time to find or use your furry soul-mate to bring positive changes and peace into your heart and mind again.

Use these questions to clarify your perceptions of your life at this point in time. Then, use your answers to write a storyline to where you want to be.

- The problem: What is your current situation?
- Your emotions: Why do you feel this way? Are you overreacting? Are you reliving conversations or events you cannot change? Are you the cause of your predicament or are you losing control over life events? Is anger or sadness keeping you from connecting with people?
- The rut: Is there a good reason you can't move on? What can you do about it? What have you tried that hasn't worked? Have you tried anything?
- Your support: Who will listen to you? Who disappointed you? Why did they disappoint you? Does anyone understand what you're going through?
- Your fears: Who can you trust? Who are your friends? Will they gossip about you or laugh behind your back? Have you become an unwilling outcast of your circle? Why?
- The starting point: What will it take for you to move forward? Do you want to move forward? What causes you to be afraid of releasing the bonds that are holding you back? Who holds you back?
- The inner you: Is your situation eating away at your self-confidence? Are you having a hard time trusting people? Do you believe you are "better off" the way you are now? Is it too hard to move forward? Would you rather subsist or exist?

In order to create positive change in your life, you must first believe it is possible to find the direction and strength within yourself. What others tell you they believe and what you know in your heart to be true can conflict. It is up to you to define what you believe and to grasp that belief to motivate yourself toward positive change to reclaim the life you had or want.

One of the best influencers to positive change is your canine companion. All pets help humans grapple with problems and show us how to effect personal positive change, but no animal spends more time with us and can accompany us to so many different places and through so many situations than a dog. It is this companion who will give you the most positive and immediate feedback and support than any other creature in the world.

If this companion is no longer at your side, it can be the most debilitating loss you can suffer. People who do not have or understand dogs do not know how important your furry friend can be. This is the child that never grows up. Is this creature Peter Pan? No, but certainly the next best thing! For people who don't have children or have never married, a canine companion is the one you can nurture and love, and he or she will do the same for you in return. Your canine companion will never betray you or talk back. He never holds a grudge and forgives willingly. He doesn't need a cellphone or prom dress. He will never borrow your car and joyride late into the night. Your every homecoming is celebrated with gusto, even if you've only left the room for a minute. He will keep you safe and monitor your health. He will listen intently to your joys and woes without judgment, and love you all the more for it.

Your dog can help you reach your goals-and the stars-together. But, what if it's the loss of your dog that is the focal point of your dilemma? Make yourself whole again by remembering how your dog was so much a part of pivotal moments you shared and, in the meantime, find that piece of heaven that your dog has left behind before he or she made their final journey across the Rainbow Bridge. Then, think about the next companion you can have to help you continue down the path to healing and positive change.

The PAWS™ System is an outgrowth of the philosophy that we all can become what we dream to be by using Pawsitive Actionable Wisdom System with which this coaching practice is derived.

2 YOUR DREAM

1. Dare to Dream

When you were a child, you had many aspirations and plans for your future. Think back and try to recall what happened to make those dreams go away. Then, think present and ask yourself if those dreams are still relevant in your life. If they are, think future and visualize one of those dreams or aspirations as part of your life. Talk to your dog about your dream. Talk about the vision or goal for that dream. Discuss the path you will take, both of you, to attain that goal. Others may tell you it's silly or impossible to chase your dream. Naysayers are always willing to tell you what's wrong with following your dream. Aren't you too old? Too young? Too small? Too weak? The only one who will believe as you do is your dog. Think of his unbridled zeal when you head down a new path, or his commiseration when you take a wrong turn. Your dog will always be there to motivate and support you. No fear or recriminations from your faithful dog!

> *You are never too old to set another goal or to dream a new dream.*
>
> -- C. S. Lewis. Author, *The Chronicles of Narnia*

Don't ever give up on your dreams. If you can't find it within yourself to dream, let your dog be the key to creating a dream for you.

-- Faith McCune

2.   Realize your Potential

Your passion, knowledge, and experience in any area of endeavor is the key to your potential. Even if you don't know where that passion, knowledge, and experience will lead, your potential will rise to the surface to show you the way. It is up to you to connect the dots between your skills and your potential. Allow your dog to help you uncover the treasures that lie beneath all the barriers you've built that keep you from realizing that potential.

Every great dream begins with a dreamer. Always remember, you have within you the strength, the patience, and the passion to reach for the stars to change the world.

-- Harriet Tubman

When you have a brand new puppy, you dream of potential, you learn patience, you develop strength to teach without anger, and you become passionate about his welfare. With time and devotion, you and your puppy can reach for the stars and change the world together.

-- Faith McCune

3.   Do What You Love

If your childhood dreams no longer hold the passion you had early on, find something that will revive the passion in your heart. Look at your dog. Does that furry creature stimulate some emotional tug in your heart? What is it you see? It could be something as simple as finding a fun activity that can help you lose a few pounds or make some new friends.

> *The question for each man to settle is not what he would do if he had means, time, influence and educational advantages; the question is what he will do with the things he has. The moment a young man ceases to dream or to bemoan his lack of opportunities and resolutely looks his conditions in the face, and resolves to change them, he lays the corner-stone of a solid and honorable success.*
>
> -- Hamilton Wright Mabie,
> American Essayist

> *Be positive in all aspects of your life. Taking out the garbage is a chore, but your dog thinks those short outings to the curb with you are magical.*
>
> -- Faith McCune

4.   Be Passionate

Have you noticed that days drag on, work is drudgery, or social events are stressful if you aren't happy? Every day can be beautiful. You will never work a day in your life if you love what you do. Celebrate your successes.

The virtue lies in the struggle, not in the prize.

-- Richard Monckton Milnes

Have you ever noticed when a dog dreams? Whether he gets what he's after is not what's important. It's the chase!

-- Faith McCune

5.   Paint a Picture

In order to clearly see the goal or dream you want to achieve, you should visualize the aftermath of the work you did to attain the result you wanted. Don't just "see" this picture in your mind, write it down. Clip a photo or draw a picture of your vision. It will set the tone for your dream and help you stay on track over the long-term, through good times or challenging ones.

Far away in the sunshine are my highest aspirations. I may not reach them, but I can look up and see their beauty, believe in them, and try to follow where they lead.

-- Louisa May Alcott,
author of Little Women

There's never a better time than when you have a new puppy to envision all the things you will do and see together in his lifetime. Start from the very first day and visualize your perfect dog. Soon enough, you'll see how perfect your dog has become. Aren't you the special parent?

-- Faith McCune

6.   Focus on the Big Picture

Once you determine what you want to do with your vision, outline the path you will take to get you to your goal. Don't let short-term obstacles stand in your way or divert you from your long-term vision.

> *Our plans miscarry because they have no aim. When a man does not know what harbor he is making for, no wind is the right wind.*
>
> -- Lucius Annaeus Seneca, Roman Statesman

> *There's never a ball thrown too far or too high for your dog to fetch. Practice your dog's technique and make it yours.*
>
> -- Faith McCune

7.   Think Big

What is a dream if you can't dream big? That dream is the big goal, but it takes incremental steps to get there. If you stop at the first step, that wasn't much of a dream at all. Go for it all. Do it all. One step at a time.

> *Cherish your visions and your dreams, as they are the children of your soul, the blueprints of your ultimate achievements.*
>
> -- Eleanor Roosevelt

*When your dog scampers away down an unknown path,
would you follow him, or abandon him? Dreams are the
same way. If you love and trust your dreams the way you
do your dog, you will follow him without question.*

-- Faith McCune

8.   Don't Look Back

Do you ever catch yourself saying, "I wish I did this," or "why
didn't I say that?" The time for looking back has passed. Do
you know that dogs live in the moment? That's why they
forgive so readily and forget about past transgressions that, in
the whole scheme of things, mean nothing. Yes, you must learn
from your mistakes and experiences, but you must also learn
not to dwell on events or words you can't change. Instead, you
must build a foundation from your mistakes and experiences
and use the knowledge you've gained to help realize the dreams
and visions you've had for yourself all along.

It's the same with every dog you have. Build on what you've
learned from one so you can provide more for the next. Thus,
not only the new dog will benefit, but so will you.

*No longer forward nor behind
I look in hope and fear;
But grateful take the good I find,
The best of now and here.*

-- John G. Whittier

Have you ever noticed how a dog lives in the moment?
All feelings of anger, fear, loneliness, or jealousy can be
dispelled with the toss of a ball or the tiniest treat. Oh,
to find that kind of bliss for ourselves.

-- Faith McCune

9. No Excuses

Do you talk yourself out of doing things? It's easy to change the course of a moment or a day by saying, "I can't," or "I don't have time." What about, "I'm afraid?" What's the worst that can happen with these excuses? Lack of action. Lack of experience. Lack of courage. Why would you want to do that to yourself?

Evidence is conclusive that your self-talk has a direct
bearing on your performance.

-- Zig Ziglar, Motivational Speaker

If you were in danger, would your dog hesitate to defend
you? Would he say, "I can't" or "I don't have time?"
He may say, "I'm afraid," but he would not allow that
fear to make him hesitate to put your welfare before his.

-- Faith McCune

10. Change your Circumstances

How often do you tell yourself, "if I only had time," or "if only this happened"? If there's a roadblock keeping you from what you really want to do, make changes. Often, what really creates the opportunity is a change in your own mindset.

Very often a change of self is needed more than a change of scene.

-- Arthur Christopher Benson,
British Author

Does your dog think, "If I only had the time," or "if only this happened" when you pick up his leash for a walk? If your dog is able to change course at a moment's notice, you are, too!

-- Faith McCune

11. Have an Unstoppable Attitude

Do you ever have mornings where just waking up is a chore? Maybe it's something you have to do that puts you in a funk (like going to the dentist for a root canal?), but it could be exhaustion or a cold. Whatever the cause, your lack of spirit and energy will make each task that much harder to do. If you pull your shoulders back and meet your challenges head-on, nothing will seem as formidable as you think. Make yourself unstoppable! Believe that you can defeat your negative thoughts and push back your doubts and/or fears with strength and determination. After all, you really are unstoppable!

You need to overcome the tug of people against you as you reach for high goals.

-- George Patton, General

For a dog, there's no such thing as a bad day. Wake up and feel the glee and joy of the moment with him. It'll brighten your day and give you the inspiration to do great things.

-- Faith McCune

12. Have Courage

Everyone has fears when learning a new task. Let's face it. Humans sabotage themselves all the time. We talk ourselves out of something we want because we don't believe we deserve it. Stop feeding yourself this propaganda. You wouldn't think about it in the first place if you weren't capable of doing it.

I learned that courage was not the absence of fear, but the triumph over it. The brave man is not he who does not feel afraid, but he who conquers that fear.

-- Nelson Mandela, Civil Rights Leader

Fear stops us from trying something new. Your dog won't allow you that privilege.

-- Faith McCune

13. Believe

Our greatest strength is inside of us. It's in our power to make our beliefs become truths. Many of us have never practiced using this strength. It's there, but you need to practice. Strength is developed through repetition. Ask any athlete. You must be athletic in your mindset. Believe in your dreams, visions, and desires. When it becomes second-nature, your belief isn't so hard to manage after all.

What lies behind us and what lies before us are tiny matters compared to what lies within us.

-- Ralph Waldo Emerson

Discovering your dog's potential is one thing. Discovering yours along the way is the best thing.

-- Faith McCune

14.   Just Do It

There is never a better time to do something you're passionate about than now. If you've ever dared yourself to jump out of a plane or off a high diving board, you know there are only two outcomes. Either you do it, or you don't. The longer you contemplate the situation, the more your brain will tell you it's not a good idea. If you don't do it, your life will remain unchanged. If you do it, your life will never be the same again. So, instead of hesitating, why not just do it?

Our doubts are traitors, and make us lose the good we oft might win, by fearing to attempt.

-- William Shakespeare

If you're afraid of dogs, you will never experience the
awesomeness of this loyal pet. Find someone who will
help you reach out to a dog and learn the secrets that lie
in those wondrous eyes and loving heart.

-- Faith McCune

15.   The Power Within You

I'm sure you've heard the term "mind over matter," but did you
know you have the power to control your aspirations by
spending a few moments each day, or night, to communicate
with your subconscious mind what you want, what your
challenges are, and where you want to be? Use this opportunity
to let your subconscious mind work for you.

The real voyage of discovery consists not in seeking new
landscapes but in having new eyes.

-- Marcel Proust

There is no boundary for your imagination when you
have a dog at your side. Explore and discover together
what glorious plans your dog has for you!

-- Faith McCune

3 ATTAINING IT

16.   Have a Plan

The one caution about dreams is they tend to put your head in the clouds thinking about how wonderful your life will be once you achieve the end results. Don't forget, you need to plan ahead in order to make your dream or goal a reality. Hard work is the first order of any dream. Just as you need to train your new puppy how to respect the rules of your home and your lifestyle, it's the same for your dream or goal. If you know what you want, you must plan all the steps it will take for you to achieve it; then, work every day toward your dream. Teaching your dog new skills demands the same kind of effort. Just because you taught your dog how to sit once, you can't expect to move on to a new skill without continued repetition and improvement on the last. It's the same with your dream. Take one step and build on it with the next to grow that solid foundation you need to make your dream a success.

You cannot dream yourself into a character: you must hammer and forge yourself into one.

-- Henry D. Thoreau

New tricks aren't learned in a day. The more you put into practice, the more proficient you will become. Your dog has the patience to wait for you to get catch up. And, you will.

-- Faith McCune

17.   Set Realistic Goals

We don't go out to conquer the world in a day. The best way to reach your ultimate goal is to break down your tasks and projects into tiny pieces. That way there is cause to celebrate every time you complete a step toward your goal. It also allows you to feel the success, and motivate yourself to continue your march to the next step, and the next, until you finally arrive where you want to be.

We cannot do everything at once, but we can do something at once.

-- Calvin Coolidge, 30th U.S. President

Your puppy is a clean slate. How you teach your puppy new skills is the way he will eventually teach you yours. Take small steps. Make it fun. Learn that happiness can be found with small successes.

-- Faith McCune

18.   Understand Your Goals

No one knows your goals better than you. Regardless of the size of your goal, it is time to clearly define what you want in your life. Once you set a goal, it's up to you to focus on the steps that you need to take to achieve it.

> *People with goals succeed because they know where they're going.*
>
> -- Earl Nightingale, Motivational Speaker

> *When you have a puppy, you want it to be well-behaved and social. Success with these goals, as in life, depends on your own desires and ingenuity. Expert advice and treats come in handy, too.*
>
> -- Faith McCune

19.   Timing is Everything

There are days when nothing seems to work. Frustration sets in and you want to just grab a surf board and head to the beach. That may be a good thing. Sometimes, getting away from your work will spark inspiration. Stepping away may be just what you need to clear your mind of clutter and get you back on track. On the other hand, you need to recognize that forcing something to happen before its time won't give you the result you want. Just keep your vision in perspective when trying to achieve what's in front of you.

Long-range goals keep you from being frustrated by short-term failures.

-- J.C. Penney, Retailer

You and your dog need moments to rest, too. Whether you're in the middle of hiking a long arduous trail or practicing your skills together. Dogs don't believe in "all work and no play." Neither should you.

-- Faith McCune

20. Get Excited to Learn

Every day brings an opportunity to learn something new. Don't take these opportunities for granted, even if the lessons are not happy or pleasant. Your experiences all hold value, especially if you can use it as a teaching moment for someone else.

Learning is a treasure that will follow its owner everywhere.

-- Proverb

Happy is the dog who plays with his master. You can teach your dog something new every day and, in the course of his education, you expand yours.

-- Faith McCune

21.   Be Serious

By being serious about your dreams and goals, you develop a
will to persist that cannot be overcome by little bumps in the
road. Keep your eye on the results you want and everything else
will fall into place.

> *Concentration can be cultivated. One can learn to*
> *exercise will power, discipline one's body and train one's*
> *mind.*
>
> -- Anil Ambani, Billionaire

> *Your dog is a willing participant in your goals and*
> *dreams. Be serious about what you teach your dog by*
> *holding yourself accountable for the results you achieve.*
>
> -- Faith McCune

22.   Know your Limitations

Sometimes, you unknowingly place too many goals on your
plate at one time. Often, tasks are not completed because
something occurs that is out of your control, or you are just
plain fatigued. Give yourself the benefit of extra time to
complete your tasks. Putting too much pressure on yourself can
be demotivating; whereas, little successes help to build your
confidence and provide moments to celebrate. Ease up on your
timelines. Be kind to yourself. Keep your eye on your dream
and it will all work out in the end.

The greatest men sometimes overshoot themselves, but then their very mistakes are so many lessons of instruction.

-- Tom Browne, American Jazz Trumpeter

Your dog will teach you efficient limitations. People find an hour is a normal amount of time to spend on projects, training, or social events. However, dogs learn best in short segments. Teaching your dog something new can be done in five minutes. Practice, praise, reward. Repeat. That's how they do it. Why not you?

-- Faith McCune

23.   Make the Process an Adventure

Look at your goals and let your passion and determination flow. If you love what you do, every day is an adventure. Every successful experience gives you the impetus to do more. Be positive, even when you're met with challenges or outright failure. Those experiences will provide you with the building blocks to invent or discover new successes in the future.

Life is either a daring adventure or nothing.

– Helen Keller

Every new day is an adventure for your dog. The anticipation of a well-worn routine is just as good as a completely new experience. Especially, when your dog is experiencing it with you. How much fun is that?

-- Faith McCune

24.   Create Opportunities

If you ever feel your ideas are running dry, think outside the box. Someone may say something that sparks your imagination with an "outlandish" idea. Don't dismiss those thoughts. Your mind is teaching you how to explore new ways to get to your goal. Those ideas are as good as gold. Spend it wisely.

> *Within our dreams and aspirations we find our opportunities.*
>
> -- Sugar Ray Leonard, boxer

> *Your dog will not leave you alone for a very long time. His insistent nudges or winsome glances will draw you away from your work to have some fun and learn something new. Spend his time wisely.*
>
> -- Faith McCune

25.   Don't Settle for Second Best

Whatever your dream or goal, you should believe you are the best and you deserve the best. By believing in yourself, you will open doors and channels, physically and mentally, to make your dreams and goals a reality. State aloud every day that you believe in your dream. Don't let others hinder your beliefs. Don't talk yourself out of it either. Ask for the means to make your dream possible. Do you think this is just whimsy? Not so! It happens every day to people just like you. The only difference is they know they are capable of reaching their dream. They don't settle for second best. Neither should you.

All parents believe their children can do the impossible. They thought it the minute we were born, and no matter how hard we've tried to prove them wrong, they all think it about us now. And the really annoying thing is, they're probably right.

-- Cathy Guisewite, Cartoonist

Who, of all living creatures, believes in you more than your dog? Yes, a lot of people come close, but your dog hangs on your every word, lingers at your side, licks you with appreciation, and waits patiently for your return. You are a miracle in your dog's eyes. How else would it be? He's the best judge of character.

-- Faith McCune

26.   Set Daily Goals

Every day, you must work a little toward your goal. If you don't, no one else will do it for you and every day you set your goals aside will be another day you won't reach them. How much time do you think you have? Make the most of every day. Make an impact every day.

If I had to select one quality, one personal characteristic that I regard as being most highly correlated with success, whatever the field, I would pick the trait of persistence.

-- Richard DeVos, Amway Co-founder

*Your dog may have the same goal every day, yet he
pursues it with vigor. You owe it to your dog to do the
same.*

-- Faith McCune

27.   Develop Good Habits

Good habits are important in everything you do. In order to do
something well you need to create standards for yourself.
Continue to read, research, and learn. In other words, gather
knowledge regularly to be at the top of your game.

Energy and persistence conquer all things.

-- Benjamin Franklin, Inventor

*Your good habits rub off on your dog. If you perform
your tasks precisely, so will he. Champions are the result
of good habits.*

-- Faith McCune

28.   Break Bad Habits

On the other side of the coin, bad habits can cause all the work
of your good habits to go away. With every good habit you
forge, give up or change a bad habit. These are the obstacles
that stand in your way from being truly successful.
Acknowledge them for what they are, then work to remove
them from your life.

Being miserable is a habit. Being happy is a habit. The choice is yours.

-- Tom Hopkins, sales trainer

Your puppy used to love gnawing at your hand when he was little. Now that he's bigger, it's not so cute anymore. Teaching your dog to break this habit will make you happier. Training for success means more treats for your dog. What could be better than that?

-- Faith McCune

29.   Keep it Lean

Learning new behaviors and tasks take time. You don't need to learn everything at once. In fact, trying to do so can be a detriment to your success. There's nothing wrong with taking baby steps.

The ability to simplify means to eliminate the unnecessary so that the necessary may speak.

-- Hans Hoffmann,
abstract expressionist painter

Your dog won't learn "sit," "stay," "down," and "come" in a day. He's not into working that hard. Focus on one thing at a time, a little at a time.

-- Faith McCune

30. Don't Neglect Things

When you set priorities, make sure you take into account all the pieces that help you to manage your priorities successfully. One small task forgotten becomes a larger task tomorrow. Eventually, your priority will take a back seat to the task you neglected. It then becomes a barrier to your own progress.

Never neglect an opportunity for improvement.

-- Sir William Jones

You have a dog. Your responsibility is to care for this dog. What moral dilemma will you face when you neglect your dog for even one day? Being accountable to him will help you be accountable to yourself and your own projects.

-- Faith McCune

31. Allot Adequate Time

We hear a daily mantra, "I don't have time!" That becomes an easy excuse for not doing what we need or want to do. Everyone has twenty-four hours each day to fill. Organize your thoughts and actions to accommodate schedule changes or delays. Stress does nothing but steal more time. Be kind to yourself. Plan ahead so you *will* have time.

You will never "find" time for anything. If you want time, you must make it.

-- Charles Buxton

Your dog is a social animal. He will take advantage of every moment he can have with you. Consider the time he spends waiting for you. The least you can do is compensate him for his patience. Don't begrudge those moments. The joy you receive when you play with your dog will re-energize you for everything else you need to accomplish.

-- Faith McCune

32.   Don't Procrastinate

Procrastinating is the same as neglecting tasks. These tasks get done "on time," just not as quickly or effectively as you would've preferred. Sometimes, procrastination is not a product of laziness, but of fear or self-doubt. Squandering away valuable time because of your own fears makes your self-talk "right," but it won't make you happy. Make a list of the types of tasks you tend to delay doing. Analyze the reason why these tasks make you procrastinate. Once you figure out what's behind the delays, dive in and work on all your tasks with equal enthusiasm and chase away those demons that cause you to procrastinate.

The whole of life is but a moment of time. It is our duty, therefore to use it, not to misuse it.

-- Plutarch

The best way to learn the consequences of procrastination is to spend a day caring for a puppy. Vigilance means one timely minute to take the little critter out or five minutes to clean up the mess. Your choice.

-- Faith McCune

4 THE DETAILS

33. Don't Make Hasty Decisions

Weigh the pros and cons of an important decision. The first option may not be the best one. Take your time. Do your research so you can make an educated decision. Get advice, but don't let people talk you into making a decision you intuitively feel is risky or wrong. Take time to study your choices. It's human to make poor choices. Those can be corrected. You just don't want to make costly ones. Being well-informed and prepared will keep your risks to a minimum.

> *Take time to deliberate, but when the time for action has arrived, stop thinking and go in.*
>
> – Napoleon Bonaparte

> *One of the hardest decisions you'll ever make is when your pet is terminally ill. How do you define "quality of life?" Are you making the right decisions for your dog or for yourself? When do you know it's time to let go? Listen to your dog. You'll find the decision wasn't yours to make after all.*
>
> -- Faith McCune

34. Raise your Standards

There are days when you don't want to do more than "just enough." How you feel and perform today could make a huge difference in your results tomorrow. Always try to do your best even when it's difficult. You never know if this is the day when something or someone very important to your success may appear. You need to be ready.

> *The greater danger for most of us lies not in setting our aim too high and falling short, but in setting our aim too low and achieving our mark.*
>
> -- Michelangelo

> *When you have a dog, you expect certain behaviors that conform to your lifestyle. You teach your dog what is acceptable and what is not. Why do you aim for perfection from your dog and not expect the same of yourself?*
>
> -- Faith McCune

35. Attitude

Being happy and passionate in your work is a big factor in your long-term success. As important as that is, you should also surround yourself with people who have the same attitude as you. Striving for success takes a positive attitude, even in tough times. Push away negative thoughts. You can never fail if you treat every mistake as a learning experience.

I believe in me more than anything in this world.

-- Wilma Rudolph, Olympic runner

Ever notice every dog has swagger? Why not you?

-- Faith McCune

36. Want Versus Need

Strive for success because you want it, not because you need it. Wanting means you intend to achieve something good and you will act to make it happen. Needing comes from scarcity. Need causes worry, stress, and pain. Want is like a beam of light that, if you focus completely on it, will show you the quickest path to your goals.

It is better to die on your feet than to live on your knees.

-- Dolores Ibarruri, Spanish revolutionary

Do you want a dog or need one? When you want one, you are opening the door to a life full of potential. If you need one, you are suffering so much that only a dog can bring you out of the abyss. It's not a bad thing to need a dog. Sometimes, you just can't do it alone.

-- Faith McCune

37. When in Doubt

There are days when you will feel the stresses and strains of a goal that seems too large to manage. Whether these cracks that appear in your foundation are driven by finances, naysayers, or self-doubt, believe that you are the only person who can do what you do. Move forward, knowing that if you don't proceed, no one else can step in and take your place, and the world will never see your greatness.

> *Inaction breeds doubt and fear. Action breeds confidence and courage. If you want to conquer fear, do not sit home and think about it. Go out and get busy.*
>
> -- Dale Carnegie

> *When your dog has doubts about doing something unfamiliar, it is up to you to coax him to try. It is also up to you to give him positive reinforcement and possibly a treat or two that says, "Good job!" He deserves it for being brave. The same goes for you.*
>
> -- Faith McCune

38. Be Proactive

Success is built on action. Be the first one to do anything. If you can't be the first, keep chipping away until you are. If there are people who you know would be great supporters of your cause, tell them what you're doing. Seek them out first. Don't wait for them to find you.

> *No great performance ever came from holding back.*
>
> – Don Greene, performance coach

A dog will never be caught off-guard. Notice how the slightest sound will cause him to run to you, then ahead in hot pursuit of that ball or leash when he knows it's "his time?" "Me first!" is his motto. Make it yours, too.

-- Faith McCune

39.   Make the Best of Each Day

Every day is filled with ups and downs. That's life. No matter how bad a day can be, always look for something positive in what has occurred. Make each challenge or disappointment a lesson that builds success for the next day.

Men's best successes come after their disappointments.

– Henry Ward Beecher

So, your dog ate your best slippers. The sky isn't falling, it's not the end of the world, and you get to buy a new pair of shoes. Just because your dog thinks your feet smell heavenly!

-- Faith McCune

40.   Give 100% Effort

There will be many moments in your journey to your goal that you will go through the motions of doing a passable job to move forward. Rather than waste time and effort, either make the sacrifice to give 100% of yourself or take a short break and reassess what you are doing. You need to do the best you can when you are working toward your goal, but if staying focused isn't working well, reassess, then get moving again. Time will not stand still. Neither should you. Don't settle for mediocrity. Remember you are doing what you love. Prepare to seek out your own level of perfection in every task you do. Even if it means taking a small step back to take a big leap forward.

> *What you lack in talent can be made up with desire, hustle and giving 110% all the time.*
>
> – Don Zimmer, Baseball Manager

> *Give your dog a bone to chew. His power of concentration on his job is enviable. His determination to finish his job, no matter how long it takes, says a lot about what 100% effort means. Take a lesson from your dog.*
>
> -- Faith McCune

41.   Be Consistent

Promise yourself that you will keep your own good counsel when it comes to rules. Once you determine what you want and how you will accomplish it, don't let behaviors or situations slide because it's convenient. Rules can always change if they aren't optimal, but until you feel justified in changing a rule, don't waver because it's too hard, or you just aren't up to honing in on your target. Slacking in one area will lead you to slack in others.

> *Perfection consists not in doing extraordinary things, but in doing ordinary things extraordinarily well.*
>
> -- Angelique Arnauld, Abbess of Port-Royal

> *Like training a dog, no improvement will occur if you aren't consistent with your own behavior. Don't change the rules. If you don't know what you want, how do you expect your dog to know?*
>
> -- Faith McCune

42. Be Logical

Rome was not built in a day. Neither will your vision or goal. Be thoughtful about every step you make toward your goal. Is it practical? Are you getting ahead of yourself? What other options are there? Use the analytical side of you to clean out the detritus your runaway creative side has produced. By seeking clarity in all the directions before you, logic will build the shortest path for you to your goal.

> *The imagination exercises a powerful influence over every act of sense, thought, reason--over every idea.*
>
> – Latin Proverb

> *If you are having trouble teaching your dog a skill, try thinking as he would. Logic, at its most basic level, is simple.*
>
> -- Faith McCune

43. Be Independent

Don't look to others to fulfill your needs. Be proactive in every task you do. It's your goal, your vision, your desire to be free of the current burdens you are experiencing. Do what is right for you without letting others influence or redirect you down a path that isn't where you want to be.

> *All life is a chance. The person who goes farthest is the one who is willing to do and dare.*
>
> — Dale Carnegie

> *Take a stand. Look at your dog and know that your show of independence is mirrored in his eyes. He'll be with you every step of the way.*
>
> -- Faith McCune

44.   Improve Efficiency

Always search to find a better way to do things. The more efficient you become, the better job you will do, and the faster you will go to reach your goal. Be protective of your time and energy. Honor your own time and make sure others respect your time as well.

> *Every day do something that will inch you closer to a better tomorrow.*
>
> — Doug Firebaugh

> *Skills are learned with repetition. When you practice skills with your dog, not only is he getting better. So are you. That's the ultimate goal, isn't it?*
>
> -- Faith McCune

45. Be a Problem Solver

There is always going to be another challenge when you are working toward your goal. There are few periods where everything runs smoothly. You are the best person to find solutions to your problems. Let your creativity take over when you feel stumped. You'll be surprised how inventive you truly are.

> *I am grateful for all of my problems. After each one was overcome, I became stronger and more able to meet those that were still to come. I grew in all my difficulties.*
>
> — J.C. Penney

> *There is no such thing as an unsolvable problem when it comes to training your dog. If you're stumped, ask your dog. Inevitably, he is the one who will train you.*
>
> -- Faith McCune

46. Be a Strong Leader

The only way to become a leader is to have a follower. No one wants to follow a weak or indecisive leader. Believe in the road you travel and the passion that is in your heart. Your belief and passion is the best metric to leading others. Helping your followers achieve their goals and encouraging them when they misstep are other ways you can become the exceptional leader you want to be.

Leadership: The art of getting someone else to do something you want done because he wants to do it.

– Dwight D. Eisenhower

If your passion and compassion are on equal levels, your dog will learn the skills you want. You may think you are the leader, but to him, he's your guide to bigger and better things. No one explores better than your dog.

-- Faith McCune

47. Guard your Emotions

It's good to be passionate about what you do and what your goals are, but be careful not to let your emotions get in the way of logic or good sense. Often, we think negative feelings like anger or disappointment are the emotions we should keep at bay. However, being overly-positive can also have a negative result. Keep an even keel when dealing with others. Being neutral can open doors for others to spread their own wings and help you fly.

You must look into other people as well as at them.

– Lord Chesterfield

A dog's sense is a great barometer of people and situations. Let him be your weather vane. You manage the rest.

-- Faith McCune

48.   Face your Weaknesses

Everyone has weaknesses. Others have strengths where you may be lacking. Seek out those people. Learn how to incorporate what they do with what you can do. Strive to make your weaknesses turn into strengths by observing, educating yourself, and practicing new skills. Find a way to make these exercises fun so you will enjoy working on your weaknesses.

> *Everywhere man blames nature and fate, yet his fate is mostly but the echo of his character and passions, his mistakes and weaknesses.*
>
> – Democritus

> *If there is a skill you cannot achieve alone, always look to others for help. Your dog is the first one who will step up to take over the reins.*
>
> -- Faith McCune

49.   Get Past Fear of Failure

The greatest obstacle to success isn't failure, but the fear of failure. Many people avoid stepping out of their comfort zones by procrastinating or avoiding tasks that could be relatively mundane to others. Fear of failure stems from self-doubt. Stop believing that "evil twin" in you that says you can't or won't, or any other millions of excuses that keep you from acting. Failure is not a bad thing. Inaction because of your fear of failure is. Cut your tasks into manageable chunks and start slicing away the layers that you can do. Very soon, you will see your task wasn't so scary after all.

*The greatest mistake you can make in life is to
continually be afraid you will make one.*

– Elbert Hubbard

*Dogs have fears, but fear of failure isn't in his nature.
He will try anything with your gentle coaxing and
encouragement because he trusts you. The same holds
true for you. If you take the first step, your dog will coax
and encourage you to take more. Trust him.*

-- Faith McCune

50. Accept Responsibility

It's easy to accept credit when it's due. Some people also accept
credit when it isn't due. Just be sure you accept responsibility
for everything you do. Honesty and integrity go hand in hand.
If you accept responsibility for your actions, honesty and
integrity will be a grasp away. Being accountable when no one
is looking is the best measure of accepting responsibility for
your own actions.

*The happiest people in the world are those who feel
absolutely terrific about themselves, and this is the
natural outgrowth of accepting total responsibility for
every part of their life.*

– Brian Tracy, author

Take responsibility for every action and interaction you make with your dog. Sometimes, you make mistakes. Don't worry. He'll forgive you for them.

-- Faith McCune

51. Don't Blame

More time is wasted by playing the blame game. It's easy to point the finger at someone else, but inevitably, the only person who is really to blame is you. Not because you did something wrong, but the finger-pointing has created a spiral of lost time, lost energy, more stress, and no action toward your goal. Be more productive with your time and yourself.

The superior man blames himself. The inferior man blames others.

– Don Shula, football coach

Blaming your dog for something you did is unconscionable. He knows the truth, but can't complain. He'll forgive you, but can you live with your actions?

-- Faith McCune

52. No Shortcuts

Shortcuts have a place in life, but not if you want to create a solid foundation for your goals. Take the time to do things right now so an incidental shortcut doesn't come back to haunt you later.

The happiness of most people we know is not ruined by great catastrophes or fatal errors, but by the repetition of slowly destructive little things.

-- Ernest Dimnet,
French priest, writer and lecturer

Do things right the first time. You'll be less likely to confuse your dog when consistent commands and action are easily recognizable from the onset.

-- Faith McCune

53. Don't Give Up

Life will happen regardless of what you do. Sometimes, the challenges put in front of you can derail the drive or momentum you have created. Even if you are forced to stop for a while, don't give up on your dream. When you do, you'll discover that phrases such as "I don't have time," "it's too late," or "I'm too old now" are just excuses. All this will add up to, "I regret." Don't quit on your dream. You'll have detours, but as long as you keep the dream alive, you'll find a way to make it become a reality.

We must all suffer from one of two pains: the pain of discipline or the pain of regret. The difference is discipline weighs ounces while regret weighs tons.

– Jim Rohn, motivational speaker

When life throws you a curve ball, don't duck. Chase it!
If you can't, your dog will show you how.

-- Faith McCune

54. Stay Motivated

Working toward a dream that only you can fathom can be a lonely job. Find passion and joy in every day, even through the most challenging times. Use laughter to lighten your burdens. There is always a glimmer of light in the darkest moments. You just need to allow your mind to find it.

When you believe and think "I can," you activate your
motivation, commitment, confidence, concentration and
excitement - all of which relate directly to achievement.

– Dr. Jerry Lynch, sports psychologist

You will always have a partner down this lonely
challenging road. Your dog will share your burden and
be the glimmer of light you need when you find it difficult
to go on.

-- Faith McCune

55. Stop Complaining

Complaining does nothing to get a task done. All it does is create negative thoughts and feelings that bring stress and dissatisfaction. You don't want to be unhappy. It's the biggest demotivator and time waster. Always look for the silver lining in all the difficulties you face. If nothing else, it is a learning moment that will teach you how strong you really are.

We are always complaining that our days are few, and acting as though there would be no end to them.

-- Lucius Annaeus Seneca, Philosopher

When your dog has a bad day, he doesn't complain. He takes it in stride and moves on. Learning to live in the moment can be a real blessing.

-- Faith McCune

56. Toxic Poisoning

Your worst enemy is not the most toxic person in your life. Some of your most well-meaning friends and/or family members can be the greatest obstacles to your success. The more they care about you, the more they don't want to see you get hurt or fail, but by coddling you at your weakest moments, they are actually chipping away at your dream. Take stock of what people are really saying, but gather the inner strength you have to keep moving toward your goals. It may not be as far away as you think.

When everybody tells you that you are being idealistic or impractical, consider the possibility that everybody could be wrong about what is right for you.

-- Gilbert Kaplan, American businessman

When you're on the verge of quitting whatever you are pursuing, talk to your dog. His wag is the best advice, encouragement, and motivation for you to continue your quest. Having someone believe in you and your goals is paramount to your inevitable success.

-- Faith McCune

57.   Time/Resource Management

One of the most difficult tasks in your life is to manage your time. It is so easy to get sidetracked by little things. You may have plans to complete a big project. You have set aside two hours. You settle in, but now you need a beverage or a snack before you start. You settle back in and get a phone call. After the call, you realize you need to pay a bill. You pop in to check your email before getting down to work. Now you look for your notes that you thought you'd placed "right here" on your desk, but can't find the folder. All of a sudden, an hour has gone by and you haven't done any of your project. You feel a little defeated as you try to get into the project again, but it just isn't that much fun anymore since you really needed the two hours to get things moving.

It's the same with resources. If you plan ahead and make sure everything you need is in place before you start your project, you will be well on your way for a successful moment in your day. Plan wisely and stay focused. You always do better if you are prepared.

Until we can manage time, we can manage nothing else.

-- Peter F. Drucker,
Author and Management Expert

Your dog will not abide you wasting his time. If you've promised him a walk or playtime, that is what he expects and that is what you will do. He is a tough taskmaster.

-- Faith McCune

5 RELATIONSHIPS

58. Community

The pulse of your business, industry, or community will provide you with a means to be successful. Look to your own grass roots to discover the people and companies that can help you grow your business. These are the organizations like the Chambers of Commerce or local business groups that regularly meet to support, share ideas, and build relationships you would otherwise be unable to create on your own. As you familiarize yourself with these groups and organizations, you will discover that there may be national and international chapters of organizations where you can expand your current market and open wide-ranging opportunities you never thought about before.

> *The most important single ingredient in the formula of success is knowing how to get along with people.*
>
> -- Theodore Roosevelt, 26th U.S. president

Go out and meet other dog owners. You can learn so
much from other people's experiences. Discover the world
together. A canine-human bond grows deeper the more
you invest in time spent together.

-- Faith McCune

59.   Find Common Ground

The best way to introduce yourself and your business is to find
a common ground or mutual interest where you can build an
ongoing relationship. Never discount anyone you meet because,
at first glance, they may not be a direct resource for you. Don't
prejudge a connection. Your common ground could be a friend
or a hobby. Through this association, a word or comment
could trigger an opportunity you would never have seen
coming.

A stray, unthought-of five minutes may contain the event
of a life, and this all-important moment — who can tell
when it will be upon us?

-- Dean Alford

To a dog, every person is equal. He is willing to share
his love and zest for life with anyone, but his loyalty to
you is steadfast. Unless someone offers him a treat.

-- Faith McCune

60.   Seek Relationships

Business is built on relationships. When all is said and done, what you tell someone about your business may not stick in their minds, but a thoughtful word or compliment could resonate many days or even years down the road. By selling yourself as the "brand" of your business, you are creating your reputation and credibility through actions and deeds, not just slogans or sales pitches.

> *To be successful, you have to be able to relate to people; they have to be satisfied with your personality to be able to do business with you and to build a relationship with mutual trust.*

> -- George Ross, Star of The Apprentice with Donald Trump

> *When left to your own devices, stepping up to meet new people may be daunting, but take a lesson from your dog. Does he have any reservations about approaching someone to say hello or sit for a treat? If he can do it, so can you!*

> -- Faith McCune

61. Collaborate with Others

Offer your assistance or support without any expectations in return. This act can bring huge dividends for your business down the road. Even in a world where "free" may not be valued, people remember kindnesses and a helping hand that doesn't come with strings attached. Your willingness to pitch in when help is needed will leave an impression that money cannot buy. It also doesn't hurt to share a good story and laugh while you're doing this.

Purpose and laughter are the twins that must not separate. Each is empty without the other.

-- Robert K. Greenleaf,
Founder of the modern
Servant leadership movement

When you have a dog, you work as a team. Decisions you make affect him as well. You cannot be selfish when your ever-willing helper is by your side. He's the one who lightens your load with joy and laughter every day.

-- Faith McCune

62.   Seek Input

No one knows everything about how to run their business, no matter how long they've been at it. Don't be afraid to ask for advice. You learn fastest and best when you learn from others. You can avoid the mistakes they made by learning from their experiences. By sharing wisdom, you might rediscover some of your own.

When spider webs unite, they can tie up a lion.

-- Ethiopian Proverb

Does your dog's behavior have you stumped? Seek advice from people who have overcome this problem. Just by asking, you will have added a new ally and support for many things beyond just your dog's behavior.

-- Faith McCune

63.   Be a Good Listener

Talking with people can be fun, but listening can be better. Of course, you need to not only hear, but also listen to what is being said. Don't just smile as you think about what you want to say next. Take in the words, absorb the knowledge, and find ways to use it to your benefit. The best student is the one who listens well.

The more you say, the less people remember.

-- François Fénelon

Your dog is a born listener. Let him be your guide. Saying too much is like barking incessantly. Soon enough, you'll create so much noise, no one will hear you.

-- Faith McCune

64.   Participate

Sometimes, standing on the side while the action is right in front of you is not the best course to take. In order to learn and develop skills in whatever you do, you must act. By participating, you will use your entire body to learn new things. Motor skills, muscle memory, problem solving, all five senses, play a role in active participation. Regardless of your expertise or confidence, always plan to participate.

You will get all you want in life if you help enough other people get what they want.

-- Zig Ziglar

You may want to stay on the sidelines and be a spectator rather than a participant. When you have a dog as a teammate, this will not be possible. You either join in the action willingly or get yanked full-speed into it. Your choice.

-- Faith McCune

65. Talk About It

Talk about what you experience or learn. This is the best way to incorporate your new skills. If there is something important you have just learned, talking about it will take that seed of information and let it germinate into a full-grown tree that branches out more and more as you develop your thoughts around these new ideas. Input from others will only help you gather the best of what you've learned and discard what you don't need.

Everybody talks about wanting to change things and help and fix, but ultimately all you can do is fix yourself. And that's a lot. Because if you can fix yourself, it has a ripple effect.

-- Rob Reiner, director

You will never run out of people who are willing to talk about their dogs. Join in the conversation by telling them what you've learned. It will reinforce what you learned and others' comments may fortify what you already know. The true beneficiary of all that knowledge? Your dog.

-- Faith McCune

66.   Offer Praise

Take every opportunity to praise people. You don't have to fabricate praise. There will always be a moment when you can say something to someone that will make their day. Everyone wants to hear that they are appreciated. Whether it's a co-worker or a stranger you meet at the grocery store. You have the power to raise someone up. Why not take advantage of these moments? It'll make you feel good, too.

> *Three billion people on the face of the earth go to bed hungry every night, but four billion people go to bed every night hungry for a simple word of encouragement and recognition.*
>
> -- Cavett Robert,
> founder National Speakers Association

> *What is the best way to get your dog to do what you want? Praise! Always tell your dog how wonderful he is and how truly marvelous he can be. Soon, some of that shine will rub off on you. Ain't it grand?*
>
> -- Faith McCune

67.   Share your Success

When you experience success, tell people about it. Humility is great, but so is new enthusiasm about your work. Let others join in and marvel at your success with you. It is hard to accomplish what you do. This is work that others don't see. The results of your efforts are worth celebrating.

The miracle is this - the more we share, the more we have.

-- Leonard Nimoy, Actor

The greatest accomplishment is just another unrecognized milestone if you don't share the celebration. If your dog finally learns not to dig up all your plants, praise him, then tell people how you did it. You have learned a skill that is well worth sharing with others.

-- Faith McCune

.

6 EDUCATION

68. Learn a New Skill

Every day is another opportunity to learn something new. Take advantage of this. If you aren't growing, you're dying. As dire as this sounds, you have only two options. Seek to grow. Don't go through the motions of living. There is more to life than blindly trudging through a routine that doesn't excite you or make you happy.

Learning is not compulsory, but neither is survival.

-- W. Edwards Deming, quality expert

When you have a dog, your mind is always thinking about how to first keep him out of mischief, then what to do together to have a great day. Learn the skill sets for you and your dog. Then, do this in your own life. Enrichment for your dog equals enrichment for you as well.

-- Faith McCune

69.   Be Excited to Learn

Remember when you were very young and you couldn't wait to learn something new? Your mind was a sponge for knowledge. You were able to achieve much in a short time span because you were willing, able, and excited to discover new things. Somewhere along the way, our natural excitement turned into a little hesitancy and even reluctance to try something new. A little self-doubt and fear crept into the picture. Let's turn this around. Go back to your youth. Keep that same level of excitement and expect positive outcomes. Regardless of the results, your initial outlook will make the new experience fresh and stimulating.

> *Pick up a grain a day and add to your heap. You will soon learn, by happy experience, the power of littles as applied to intellectual processes and gains.*
>
> -- John S. Hart

> *When you have a dog, you have the responsibility of teaching him the skills that will make him an accepted member of your family and circle of friends. You have an eager student. Take advantage of it.*
>
> -- Faith McCune

70.   Expand your Mind

The world is full of creative minds. Let yours be one of them. Think about your goals. Imagine what you need to do to achieve them. Then, find ways to develop opportunities and relationships that will help you reach your goals. Believe that everything is within your reach. You have the ability to invent your own solutions.

It's what you learn after you know it all that counts.

-- John Wooden, basketball coach

How do you discover great activities for you and your dog? Use your creativity. Use your dog's creativity. Together, you may find a unique exercise you both love. Laughter and happiness will follow.

-- Faith McCune

71.   Read

In this time when we are all bombarded with information, we all make the mistake of reading in short segments—5, 10, 15 seconds at a time. If it doesn't seem interesting or important at the time, we dismiss it and go on to other things. What we miss is the true communication that reading a book or article from start to finish affords us. Choose a book and read it from cover to cover. If you only have a little time to read, set a goal for yourself to read for one page each day. After a year, you will have accumulated 365 pages of content you may find critical in your future projects. Knowledge is what makes you stand out above others.

Man only learns in two ways, one by reading, and the other by association with smarter people.

-- Will Rogers

If your dog could read, think about what his concerns would be. Then, find a book that applies so you can be his expert.

-- Faith McCune

72.   Seek Out Experts

What you cannot readily find in books, you can find through experts. Sometimes, these experts are your neighbors or friends. Ask questions so people can help you find your answers. You never know who that expert might be.

Bottom line: if you show a genuine interest in learning about how others became successful, you can open up a world of opportunities.

-- Armstrong Williams, Political Commentator

Every dog owner is an expert in something they are seeking. Whether it's teaching "sit" or "stay" or ways to change a quirky behavior, talking to people can be your quickest solution.

-- Faith McCune

73.   Take Classes

There is no such thing as too much education. Take a class to gain some new insights on an old subject or learn something new. Continue to grow. Every day is more exciting and fulfilling when you have places to go, things to do, and people to meet.

The wisest mind has something yet to learn.

-- George Santayana, Philosopher

Enrolling yourself and your dog in a class is a big step into the canine arena. Not only are you learning, but so is your dog. It's okay if he has to wait for you to catch up.

-- Faith McCune

74.   Attend Seminars

Have the courage to step into a larger learning curve by attending a seminar. You will meet so many people who have the same interests. Not only do you expand your knowledge, you will gain a circle of friends who have the same goals and interests you do. Keep them close as you learn. They will provide the support system you need when you run out of ideas on your own.

*I learn something new about the game almost every time
I step on the course.*

-- Ben Hogan, golfer

*Take advantage of experts who can provide more
knowledge and proficiency in your chosen activity with
your dog. Be the best that you can be!*

-- Faith McCune

75.   Conduct Research

What you cannot find through selected books, classes, and
seminars, conduct personal research to become your own
home-grown expert. Sometimes, what you're looking for can't
be found in one book or article, but several. Information is
easily accessible on the internet. Use this resource to find what
you need to stay updated and current.

*Go to the people. Learn from them. Live with them.
Start with what they know. Build with what they have.
The best of leaders when the job is done, when the task is
accomplished, the people will say we have done it
ourselves.*

-- Lao Tzu

Dog ownership is a big responsibility. Don't rely on just your own common sense to care for your pet. Get a second opinion. Do your research.

-- Faith McCune

76. Take Notes

It's prudent to have a notebook with you at all times. Bright ideas or new contacts appear randomly, never when you plan for them. Don't let great moments and opportunities slip away because you don't have a pen and paper handy. You may prefer to carry a handheld recorder or use the notes app on your cell phone. Use the method that works best for you. Once you get into the habit, you will have more ideas and opportunities to work with than before.

Nothing is more expensive than a missed opportunity.

-- H. Jackson Brown, Author

Sometimes, a great opportunity appears for you and your dog to bond. Make a note of it so you don't forget. It may lead to unforgettable moments you'll treasure for years to come.

-- Faith McCune

77. Keep a Journal

Keeping a journal is not the same as taking notes. Your journal reflects some of the thoughts and actions you experience during the day. It's a written log of your own progress toward your goals. You have an intimate "listener" to the successes and challenges you experience. You also have a place to record mistakes or embarrassing moments that you may not want to share with others. Logging these moments down can help you clear the air for yourself and even objectively dissect the situation so you don't commit the same mistakes again. Write about your successes so you can celebrate these moments again in the future. Use these moments to savor your progress or refuel yourself when times get a little rough.

> *The important thing is to learn a lesson every time you lose.*
>
> -- John McEnroe, tennis champion

> *Keeping a record of your dog's adventures may seem laborious, but one day you'll look back and see how much you've accomplished together. What a team you are!*
>
> -- Faith McCune

78. Be Open to Improvement

Never settle for less than you think you deserve. If you haven't reached your goal or are struggling to make a breakthrough, always believe that you can find a better way to do things, then go out and search for alternative solutions. If you don't have the answer, someone else might. Seek out the people you need to help you reach your goal. Do research. Take a class. Talk to people to expand the knowledge you currently have.

A man learns to skate by staggering about making a fool of himself; indeed, he progresses in all things by making a fool of himself.

-- George Bernard Shaw, Writer and Critic

Keep learning new tricks for the benefit of your dog. You may find he's smarter than you think. By expanding his horizons you're also expanding yours.

-- Faith McCune

79. Apply What You Learn

Many people spend hours, days, or years studying and researching. That's great, but if you don't act on the information you gather, you are not sharing your knowledge or expertise with others. That is a tremendous disservice to yourself and your potential audience. Everyone has something to share with others or the world. Where would we be if Thomas Edison did not share his light bulb with the world? We would still be living in darkness or candlelight. Treasure your knowledge. It may be a simple thing to you, but could mean the world to others.

The greatest achievement of the human spirit is to live up to one's opportunities and make the most of one's resources.

-- Marquis de Vauvenargues,
French writer and moralist

Which is better? Reading about how to train your dog or actually doing it? If you say "doing it," you are a wise human.

-- Faith McCune

80.   Practice Time

We've all heard the term, "practice makes perfect." We all want to be perfect. Whether we want to make a big impact or avoid embarrassing ourselves, it's important to practice. We can train ourselves to be the best at what we do. We can also assist others to be the best at what they do, too, by listening to or doing what you, the expert, tell them. You can only convince people of your expertise if you are strong and sure of your information. And, how do we do that? Practice!

Someone might have a germ of talent, but 90% of it is discipline and how you practice it, what you do with it. Instinct won't carry you through the entire journey. It's what you do in the moments between inspiration.

-- Cate Blanchett, actress

What dog would miss an opportunity to play?
Incorporate practice with play. It's all the same to him.

-- Faith McCune

81. Location, Location, Location

Whether you are a real estate agent or a stay-at-home mom, location is everything when it comes to a project worth doing. When you have a goal, you want to stretch and grow in the best situation. If you are writing a book, you need to concentrate on your content. A quiet space would probably work best. If you are gathering information about opening a bakery, you would likely seek out shops and talk to owners in the neighborhoods that are suitable to your type of pastries. Finding the best place for your work gives you a leg up in everything you do. The best environment brings out the best thinking and creating.

Little League baseball is a very good thing because it
keeps the parents off the streets.

– Yogi Berra

There are all kinds of great places to take your dog.
Walking the same path every day may bore you. Imagine
what it's like for him? Same old mail, day after day.

-- Faith McCune

7 FINANCIAL

82.   Keep Good Records

Organization in every aspect of your life and business will keep you from wasting time and money. You will also have more peace of mind by avoiding unnecessary stress. If your records are in order, you will have no problem accessing important information whenever you need it. Your reputation will get a boost for being prompt and able to do any task you are given.

> *My father taught me that reputation, not money, was the most important thing in the world.*
>
> -- William Rosenberg, Dunkin Donuts founder

> *You know everything about your dog. What if you go away for a while? Make sure your caretaker has all his records while you're gone. It's the right thing to do.*
>
> -- Faith McCune

83.   Plan your Expenditures

Budgeting and planning strategically lays out your expectations for your life and your business. If you plan ahead, you avoid many unwelcome surprises or forgotten expenses. Being knowledgeable about your expenses also creates the same peace of mind you have when you keep good records.

Happiness is not in the mere possession of money; it lies in the joy of achievement, in the thrill of creative effort.

-- Franklin D. Roosevelt, 32nd U.S. President

Just as you budget for yourself, budget for your dog, too. Put aside a little money regularly so your dog's needs aren't a burden. When times get tough, our pets could be the first to suffer.

-- Faith McCune

84.   Spend Wisely

Knowing what your priorities are will keep you from spending impulsively. That is the worst form of spending. It's unplanned, unbudgeted, and could be unnecessary. And the worst of the worst? Unreturnable. Whether it's a big expense or small, it still makes an impact on your bottom line. How unfortunate it would be to miss a great opportunity because you were short a few dollars?

The person who pays an ounce of principle for a pound of popularity gets badly cheated.

-- Ronald Reagan, 40th U.S. president

We always see great toys and treats at the pet store. It's hard to resist when they all shout, "buy me!" Resist the temptation. Your dog is happiest with his old stinky toy and "diet" isn't in his vocabulary.

-- Faith McCune

85.   Look for Value

Don't let others' perceptions change your ideas about value. Whether people see you as "cheap," frugal, thrifty, or sensible, make your own determination of perceived value for yourself. Be happy when you make a good deal. Every penny you save on one item allows you to put that penny to work for you elsewhere.

Time is more value than money. You can get more money, but you cannot get more time.

-- Jim Rohn, Motivational Speaker

When you love your dog, you always want the best for him. Price isn't the ideal indicator. Ask your friends. Seek advice. Then, make a decision with him in mind.

-- Faith McCune

8 SELF

86.   Become the Expert

Everything you learn or experience makes you unique. Whether you know it or not, you are an expert at something and someone is searching for you to be the solution to their problem. Don't belittle your knowledge. It's a gift that only you can share with the world.

> *The first step in the acquisition of wisdom is silence, the second listening, the third memory, the fourth practice, the fifth teaching others.*
>
> -- Solomon Ibn Gabriol,
> Hebrew poet and philosopher

> *After raising a dog for years, you become your dog's expert--his advocate. Be proud of this, just as he's proud of you.*
>
> -- Faith McCune

87.   Patience and Dues

Nothing will happen overnight. Patience is something you will
learn when striving to reach your goal. You also have to pay
your dues and wait your turn when there is something
important that you wish to attain. Nothing that is truly valuable
is free. Skills worth having and developing will require
dedication and sacrifice. As you progress on your journey, you
will see that patience is a virtue well worth cultivating.

> *No road is too long for him who advances slowly and
> does not hurry, and no attainment is beyond his reach
> who equips himself with patience to achieve it.*
>
> -- Jean de La Bruyère,
> French philosopher and moralist.

> *Every dog will teach you patience. Communicating with
> a dog is like learning a new language. How wonderful to
> be bilingual.*
>
> -- Faith McCune

88.   Have Balance in Your Life

Many people who start new businesses or skills tend to pour
extra effort and time into this new goal. Your passion will take
over if you don't plan to keep balance in your life. You may
sometimes wish you didn't have friends, family, or distractions
to keep you away from working on your goals, but these people
and chores give you the break you need to refresh your mind

and body so you can start another day with a clear mind. Don't begrudge the time you have with others. They are a blessing you need, even though the break may be inconvenient at the time.

> *What will your children remember? Moments spent listening, talking, playing and sharing together may be the most important times of all.*
>
> -- Gloria Gaither

> *There is no better way to have balance in your life than by having a dog. He is your friend, your support, and your conscience. He's also your alarm clock and fun police.*
>
> -- Faith McCune

89.   Take Care of Yourself

You may get lost in your projects or creative thoughts and forget to do the important things that keep your mind and body nourished. Eating regular meals, drinking water, exercising, and getting enough sleep are all critical to attaining your goals. Beyond these necessities, you must also learn to relax, enjoy companionship, and laugh. How you care for yourself reflects on how you care for others as well.

> *Set peace of mind as your highest goal, and organize your life around it.*
>
> -- Brian Tracy, Speaker, Author, Consultant

Dogs decipher human frailties quickly. If you don't take care of yourself, your dog will push you in the direction you need to go. Listen to his signals.

-- Faith McCune

90.   Avoid Stress

Be organized and methodical in your everyday life. You can avoid or divert some of the daily stresses you may experience by taking time to relax. Meditate, read, or enjoy some fresh air. Avoiding stress clears the mind of useless diversions that waste time and stir up emotions and reactions that get in the way of your progress.

Keep your sense of humor. There's enough stress in the rest of your life to let bad shots ruin a game you're supposed to enjoy.

-- Amy Alcott, golfer

Breathing is a very simple act. So is playing with your dog. Breathing and playing are equals when you need relaxation the most.

-- Faith McCune

91.   Learn How to Delegate

When you first start out on any project, you start out alone.

Once the project starts to gain momentum, you must decide who and what will help you reach your goal. Learning to delegate is a skill you need. You are only one person. In order to do a good job in anything, you need a team. Whether it's a team of one or a hundred, letting go of the reins and bringing on new team members can get the job done much quicker. You also get the benefit of partners who share a common goal and enjoy each other's company.

Many hands make light work.

-- English Proverb

Did you know there are dogs that do the work of humans? They are called service dogs. Every day, they do chores that their humans cannot do. They are highly trained, skilled dogs. They may not work for peanuts, but they won't complain about not getting a raise.

-- Faith McCune

92.   Get the Word Out

Now that you're an expert, tell people what you can do. Let others help spread the word. With just ten friends, you can reach a whole network of people who can tell other people what you do. Soon, by word of mouth, you can have a following of people with mutual interests dedicated to your expertise.

I have found that being honest is the best technique I can use. Right up front, tell people what you're trying to accomplish and what you're willing to sacrifice to accomplish it.

-- Lee Iacocca, executive

Every dog owner has unique stories about their pets. Your stories will encourage others to relate theirs. What a wonderful way to discover more skills you can adapt into your own life.

-- Faith McCune

93.   Give Yourself a Break

We are our harshest critics. Being "perfect" is not reasonable. Perfection means you have reached the pinnacle and there is nowhere to go and no improvements to make. That is certainly not where you want to be. Being the best you can be at a given moment in time is better. It gives you the latitude to make mistakes, but also to find solutions to correct or fix those mistakes so you can grow.

Failure is a trickster with a keen sense of irony and cunning. It takes great delight in tripping one when success is almost within reach.

-- Napoleon Hill

Your dog trusts you to be the best you can be, but he doesn't judge when you aren't at your best every day. Don't be perfect. Be the best you can be today. He'll love you just the same.

-- Faith McCune

94.   Take a Break

If you find yourself stuck in a rut, don't keep digging. Stop and reset your task. In computer language, "reboot." You may have too much information or you're doing too much of the same thing. If you take a breather from your task, your mind will strip away all that's unnecessary so you can get back to the core of your work.

Success is sweet, the sweeter if long delayed and attained through manifold struggles and defeats.

-- A. Bronson Alcott

You've tried and tried to teach your dog this one trick, but he just doesn't get it. Don't get frustrated and give up. Just give it a rest for a while. Your dog may just be testing you.

-- Faith McCune

95. Rewards

Everyone needs a reward. Whether it's a kind word or a night out on the town, take the time to celebrate. Every celebration means you've hit a milestone in your goal. If you have a team, include them in the celebration. Everyone needs encouragement. It's so much better when you include others in the moment.

> *To fulfill the dreams of one's youth; that is the best that can happen to a man. No worldly success can take the place of that.*
>
> -- Willa Cather

> *Every day is a celebration when you have a dog. The reward is the time you have to enjoy his company. Take him for a ride. Visit the pet store. Share a "forbidden" treat like ice cream. Who's going to tell on you? Your dog's lips are sealed—except for the creamy ring under his chin.*
>
> -- Faith McCune

96. Be Thankful

Always count your blessings. If not for an instance, circumstance, or person, that blessing may not have been yours. Where would you be without that one opportunity or referral that changed everything? Never forget those who have helped you. If you can't reciprocate, at least remember their kindness and pay it forward.

> *If I have seen further it is by standing on the shoulders of giants.*

> -- Isaac Newton

> *Be ever so thankful for the dog you have. Believe that he chose you to be his family. He came into your life to bring you joy, comfort, and even solve a problem you didn't know you had. It will be evident soon enough.*

> -- Faith McCune

97.   Be Happy

Every day is not work if you're happy. Smile and laugh whenever you can. Even when times get tough, try to find the silver lining in the situation. Nothing is quite so bad and the solutions are just a thought away if you try to find the positive side of every problem.

> *If we would see the color of our future, we must look for it in our present; if we would gaze on the star of our destiny, we must look for it in our hearts.*

> -- Canon Frederic Farrar, cleric and writer

> *Happiness can be fleeting, but is a very renewable resource when you have a dog.*

> -- Faith McCune

98.   Be Nice

It costs nothing to be nice to people. The memory you create in someone's mind is based on how you treat them, not what you know or do. Be memorable. Be nice.

I've learned that people will forget what you said, people will forget what you did, but people will never forget how you made them feel.

-- Maya Angelou, Poet

Loving a dog opens your heart to loving others without restrictions. Just like your dog, love unconditionally, forgive, and trust that your love will be reciprocated.

-- Faith McCune

99.   Have Fun

Enjoy every day like it's the best day you've ever had. If you remember to have fun whenever you can, your joy will be infectious and others will feed off your attitude. You may not change the world, but you can certainly change the lives of a few people when you're having fun.

Success is not the key to happiness. Happiness is the key to success. If you love what you are doing, you'll be a success.

-- Albert Schweitzer, humanitarian

Does your dog make you laugh? I can't say "no" with a straight face.

-- Faith McCune

100. Appreciate Life

All you receive comes from the efforts of others. When you were a child, you received everything from your parents. If you weren't fortunate enough to have nurturing parents, there is always one person who made a big impact on your life. Appreciate that person. Appreciate what that person taught you. Then, appreciate what you have done with that knowledge. Your life is special and unique. Treasure what you have. There's no one like you.

There are two things to aim at in life; first to get what you want, and after that to enjoy it. Only the wisest of mankind has achieved the second.

-- Logan Pearsall Smith, essayist and critic

We often take for granted the wonderful dog that's in our life until the happy routine is disrupted. Whether it is a little injury, health concern, or end of life, treasure the moments you have. They are gone all too soon.

-- Faith McCune

101. Repositioning and Reflection

Think about all your experiences and the people who have influenced your thoughts and actions in the past. It has made you the person you are today. How you use those experiences, thoughts, and actions determine your contribution to those around you and beyond. Never short-change your importance to the world. A few words, a kind gesture, or a helping hand can be remembered for a lifetime, whether you know it or not. That's the beauty of it all.

> *If you can dream it, you can do it. Always remember this whole thing was started by a mouse.*
>
> -- Walt Disney, Animator, Film Producer

> *In those twilight years as you hold your dog's face in your hands and look into his soft, moist eyes, remember the journey you have both traveled and see how far he has taken you without your knowing it.*
>
> -- Faith McCune

APPENDIX

CELEBRATIONS

JANUARY
National Train Your Dog Month
National Walk Your Pet Month
JANUARY 2: National Pet Travel Safety Day
JANUARY 14: National Dress Up Your Pet Day
JANUARY 24: Change a Pet's Life Day
JANUARY 29: Seeing Eye Guide Dog Birthday

FEBRUARY
Dog Training Education Month
Humane Society of the United States Spay/Neuter Awareness Month
National Pet Dental Health Month
National Prevent a Litter Month
Responsible Pet Owners Month
Unchain a Dog Month
FEBRUARY 3: St. Blaise Day (Patron saint of veterinarians and animals)
FEBRUARY 7-14: Have a Heart for a Chained Dog Week
FEBRUARY 14: National Pet Theft Awareness Day
FEBRUARY 15-21: National Justice for Animals Week
FEBRUARY 16-17: Westminster Kennel Club Annual Dog Show
FEBRUARY 20: Love Your Pet Day
FEBRUARY 22: Walking the Dog Day
FEBRUARY 23: International Dog Biscuit Appreciation Day
FEBRUARY 24: World Spay Day / Spay Day USA

MARCH
Poison Prevention Awareness Month
MARCH 1-7: Professional Pet Sitters Week
MARCH 3: If Pets had Thumbs Day
MARCH 5-8: Crufts (The World's Largest Dog Show) held in Birmingham, England
MARCH 7: Iditarod Race Starts (Awards Banquet on March 22)
MARCH 13: K-9 Veterans Day
MARCH 15-21: Poison Prevention Week
MARCH 23: National Puppy Day

APRIL

American Red Cross Pet First Aid Awareness Month
ASPCA Prevention of Cruelty to Animals Month
National Adopt a Greyhound Month
National Heartworm Awareness Month
Prevent Lyme Disease in Dogs Month
APRIL 1-7: International Pooper Scooper Week
APRIL 2: Every Day is Tag Day
APRIL 8: National Dog Fighting Awareness Day
APRIL 11: National Pet Day
APRIL 12-18: National Animal Control Officer Appreciation Week
APRIL 18: Pet Owners Independence Day
APRIL 19: Pet Owners Day
APRIL 19 25: National Pet ID Week
APRIL 19-25: Animal Cruelty/Human Violence Awareness Week
APRIL 21: Bulldogs are Beautiful Day
APRIL 23: National Lost Dog Awareness Day
APRIL 25: World Veterinary Day
APRIL 26: National Kids and Pets Day
APRIL 26: National Pet Parent's Day
APRIL 29: International Guide Dog Day
APRIL 30: National Adopt a Shelter Pet Day

MAY

ACVO Service Dog Eye Examination Month
Chip Your Pet Month
Go Fetch! National Food Drive for Homeless Animals Month
National Pet Month
MAY 1: National Purebred Dog Day
MAY 3: Mayday for Mutts
MAY 3: National Specially-abled Pets Day
MAY 3-9: National Pet Week
MAY 3-9: Be Kind to Animals Week
MAY 4-10: Puppy Mill Action Week
MAY 8: National Animal Disaster Preparedness Day
MAY 17-23: National Dog Bite Prevention Week

JUNE
National Microchip Month
National Pet Preparedness Month
Social Petworking Month
JUNE 1-7: Pet Appreciation Week
JUNE 9: World Pet Memorial Day
JUNE 19: Ugliest Dog Day
JUNE 19: National Pets in Film Day
JUNE 21: National Dog Party Day
JUNE 26: Take Your Dog to Work Day

JULY
National Dog House Repairs Month
JULY 11: All American Pet Photo Day
JULY 15: National Pet Fire Safety Day
JULY 21: National Craft For Your Local Shelters Day
JULY 31: National Mutt Day #1

AUGUST
AUGUST 1: DOGust Universal Birthday for Shelter Dogs
AUGUST 2-8: International Assistance Dog Week
AUGUST 4: National Assistance Dog Day
AUGUST 9-15: Feeding Pets of the Homeless Week
AUGUST 10: Spoil Your Dog Day
AUGUST 15: National Check the Chip Day
AUGUST 15: International / National Homeless Animals Day
AUGUST 26: National Dog Day
AUGUST 30: National Holistic Pet Day

SEPTEMBER
AKC Responsible Dog Ownership Month
National Guide Dogs Month
National Disaster Preparedness Month
SEPTEMBER 13: National Pet Memorial Day
SEPTEMBER 13: National Hug Your Hound Day
SEPTEMBER 19: Responsible Dog Ownership Day
SEPTEMBER 19: Puppy Mill Awareness Day

SEPTEMBER 20-26: National Deaf Dog Awareness Week
SEPTEMBER 20-26: Adopt a Less Adoptable Pet Week
SEPTEMBER 20-26: National Dog Week
SEPTEMBER 23: Dogs in Politics Day (also known as Checkers Day)

OCTOBER
American Humane Association Adopt a Dog Month
ASPCA Adopt A Shelter Dog Month
National Animal Safety and Protection Month
National Pit Bull Awareness Month
National Pet Wellness Month
National Service Dog Month
Wishbones for Pets Month
OCTOBER 1: National Black Dog Day
OCTOBER 4: World Animal Day
OCTOBER 4: Blessing of the Animals Day / World Animal Day
OCTOBER 4-11: National Walk Your Dog Week
OCTOBER 8: National Pet Obesity Awareness Day
OCTOBER 11-17: National Veterinary Technician Week
OCTOBER 27: National Pit Bull Awareness Day

NOVEMBER
ASPCA Adopt a Senior Pet Month
National Pet Cancer Awareness Month
National Pet Diabetes Month
National Senior Pet Month
NOVEMBER 1: National Cook for Your Pets Day
NOVEMBER 1-7: National Animal Shelter Appreciation Week

DECEMBER
DECEMBER 2: National Mutt Day #2
DECEMBER 10: International Animal Rights Day
DECEMBER 11-13: AKC/Eukanuba National Championship Dog Show
DECEMBER 22: Keep Pets Safe in Winter Day

A Dog's Creed

I was born to be a loving, forgiving, and guiding creature made in the likeness of a dog. Somewhere in the world, there is someone looking for me, someone who needs my help and love. It is my purpose to seek them out.

If I am lucky enough to find my special someone when I am very young, I will do my best to adhere to the training I am given, no matter what Nature's bidding requires. If it takes a long time to find my special someone, I will continue my search until I can seek no more.

I will give my unconditional love to those who care for me and forgive their angry words or harsh hands because I have been given a responsibility yet unknown to them. You see, my task is to guide, care for, and help my special someone to a life happier and more fulfilling than they were able to achieve on their own, before I appeared.

A life without purpose, or one lived in anger, loneliness or solitude is not the way humans were meant to be. Instead, I will lovingly engulf them with my energy, bring friends they will cherish, and share experiences they will remember for a lifetime.

But the day shall come when I must leave my special someone to advance alone. It is then I will make my journey back to where I came, over the Rainbow Bridge, to be with my own doggie friends, until I am called to do my work again.

In loving memory of Corrie, 3-1-03 to 5-16-13

Made in the USA
Charleston, SC
27 December 2015